Bats

By Eric Braun and Sandra Donovan

Raintree

ANIMALS OF THE RAINFOREST

www.raintreepublishers.co.uk

Visit our website to find out more information about Raintree books.

To order:
- ☎ Phone 44 (0) 1865 888112
- 📄 Send a fax to 44 (0) 1865 314091
- 🖥 Visit the Raintree Bookshop at www.raintreepublishers.co.uk to browse our catalogue and order online.

First published in Great Britain by Raintree Publishers, Halley Court, Jordan Hill, Oxford, OX2 8EJ, part of Harcourt Education.
Raintree is a registered trademark of Harcourt Education Ltd.

Originated by Dot Gradations Ltd
Printed and bound in Hong Kong and China by South China

ISBN 1 844 21104 5
07 06 05 04 03
10 9 8 7 6 5 4 3 2 1

British Library Cataloguing in Publication Data
Braun, Eric
Bats - (Animals of the rainforest)
1. Bats - Juvenile literature
2. Rain forest ecology - Juvenile literature
I.Title 599.4
A catalogue for this book is available from the British Library.

Acknowledgements
The publishers would like to thank the following for permission to reproduce photographs:
Corbis/Eric and David Hosking, p. **8**; Visuals Unlimited/Brian Rogers, p. **1**; Joe McDonald, pp. **6, 16, 24, 28–29**; Rob & Ann Simpson, pp.**12, 22, 26**; Bruce S. Cushing, p. **14**; Richard Thom, pp. **18, 20**; Warren Photographic, p. **5, 13, 21**; Wildlife Conservation Society/ D. Demello, p. **11**.

Cover photograph by Digital Stock.

Every effort has been made to contact copyright holders of any material reproduced in this book. Any omissions will be rectified in subsequent printings if notice is given to the publishers.

Contents

Any words appearing in the text in bold, **like this**, are explained in the Glossary.

USA

MEXICO

GUATEMALA
BELIZE
HONDURAS
EL SALVADOR
NICARAGUA
COSTA RICA
PANAMA

Caribbean Sea

North Atlantic Ocean

VENEZUELA
GUYANA
SURINAM
FRENCH GUIANA

COLOMBIA

ECUADOR

Amazon River

PERU

BOLIVIA

BRAZIL

PARAGUAY

South Pacific Ocean

URUGUAY

ARGENTINA

CHILE

South Atlantic Ocean

N
W   E
S

Range of rainforest bats
Surrounding land
Sea
Borders
Rivers

A quick look at bats

What do bats look like?
Bats come in many different sizes and are covered in fur. They come in different colours, including dark brown, silver and black.

Where do bats live?
Bats live all over the world, except where it is very cold. Many kinds of bats live in rainforests.

What do bats eat?
Most bats eat insects. Some kinds of bats eat fish, frogs, birds, scorpions, mice and even other bats. There are also bats that eat fruit, pollen and nectar from plants.

Do bats have any enemies?
Yes. Owls can snatch bats out of the sky. Snakes can climb into trees or caves to catch bats. People also kill many bats.

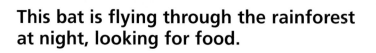
This bat is flying through the rainforest at night, looking for food.

Bats in the rainforest

Bats have been on Earth for millions of years. One of the scientific names for bats is Chiroptera (kye-ROPT-uh-ruh). This means 'hand-winged'. The wings of a bat cover the bones in its hands.

Bats are **mammals**. A mammal is a warm-blooded animal with a backbone. Warm-blooded animals have a body temperature that stays the same, even when it is hot or cold outside. One thing sets bats apart from all other mammals. They are the only mammals that can truly fly.

Bats are **nocturnal**. Nocturnal means they are active at night. Bats sleep during the day and hunt for food at night. Most bats eat insects, but some eat fruits and plants.

▲ **This spectacled flying fox is hanging upside down from a tree in the rainforest.**

Kinds of rainforest bat

Bats are important because they help keep the insect population under control. Bats are also important **pollinators** for many plants, including bananas. Pollinators are things that spread pollen. Pollen is a dusty material that plants make so that new plants can grow.

There are almost a thousand species of bat. A species is a group of animals or plants closely related to each other. Bats are divided into two main groups called megabats and microbats. Megabats are large, and microbats are small.

Most bats are microbats. Most microbats weigh less than 56.7 grams. The smallest microbat is the bumblebee bat, which is found in Thailand. It is the size of a child's fingernail and weighs less than a one-pence piece. All the bats that live in North and South America are microbats.

There are nearly two hundred species of megabat. Flying foxes are the largest of all megabats. They weigh up to 1.8 kilograms and have wingspans up to 1.8 metres.

Bats that live in the rainforest can be both beautiful and strange. A bat called the spectacled flying fox has light-coloured fur around its eyes. The fur looks like spectacles. The straw-coloured fruit bat has long, narrow wings. These wings help it to fly higher and further than most bats.

Range and habitat

Bats live all over the world, except in places where it is very cold. Many kinds of bat live in rainforests. A rainforest is a warm place where many trees and plants grow close together and a lot of rain falls. Megabats live in Asia, Australia, Africa and on some islands in the Pacific Ocean. Microbats live on every continent except Antarctica.

Bats need to live in a place where they can sleep safely during the day. Many bats like to sleep in trees. Some bats hide under the bark. Others hang upside down from the branches. They wrap themselves in their wings.

Some bats fold leaves over themselves. The leaves make a tent so the bat is hidden. One of these bats is the Honduran white bat. When hidden under a leaf, its white fur looks green to other animals. This is because the green leaf reflects on to the white.

Another place that bats live is in caves. They also live in the attics or walls of houses or other buildings. Bats live in tunnels and under bridges too.

▲ **This bat is sleeping in the rainforest. It folds its wings around itself while it rests.**

Most bats are social. They are friendly to each other. They often sleep in large groups. If a bat is in trouble, it will make a special sound that tells other bats that it is in trouble. Then, other bats will come to help it.

▲ This leaf-nosed bat has flaps of skin around its nose.

Appearance

A bat's fur can be many different colours, including dark brown, silver and black. Some bats have spots or other coloured patterns on their wings. Colours, shapes and patterns that make something blend in with its background are called **camouflage**.

Did you know that bats have their legs on backwards compared to other animals? Their knees and feet are rotated 180 degrees so that they can hang upside down against a flat surface.

Bats have different-coloured coats so they can blend in with their surroundings. This makes it difficult for their enemies to see them. Speckled bats can blend in with rock or bark. Red, orange or yellow bats can hide in fruit trees and look like ripe fruit.

Bats also have different-shaped noses. Leaf-nosed bats have flaps of skin around their noses that look like leaves.

Bats have tails of different lengths. Some of them are short and fit neatly between the bat's legs. Other tails stick out past the bat's hind legs. Some bats have no tail at all.

Bats' wings are made of a **membrane**. Each wing is made up of four long fingers and one clawed thumb. A bat's wings are attached to its hind legs. The wing membrane stretches between the hind legs. Bats use this to help them steer and stop as they fly.

This is a fishing bat. It swoops down to the water and tries to grab fish to eat.

What bats eat

Most bats eat insects. One small bat can eat up to 600 moths, mosquitoes or other insects in an hour. In Texas, there are about 20 million bats living in a cave called Bracken Cave. They are Mexican free-tail bats, and they eat about 200 tonnes of insects every night. Some kinds of bats eat fish, frogs, birds, scorpions, mice and even other bats.

There are also bats that eat pollen and nectar. Nectar is a sweet liquid found inside a plant or flower. Some bats have long noses. They can poke them deep into flowers to find pollen to eat.

Most megabats eat fruit. The straw-coloured fruit bat and the Jamaican leaf-nosed fruit bat like to eat figs, mangos, avocados and bananas. The straw-coloured fruit bat can chew into the hard covering of a coconut.

▲ **These bats are eating bananas.**

After they eat

Most fruit-eating bats cannot digest the seeds in the fruits they eat. Digest means to break down food so the body can use it. These seeds leave the bats in their waste. Waste is undigested food that leaves an animal's body in droppings. Some of the seeds grow into new trees.

How do bats find food?

While hunting for food at night, bats make a series of high-pitched sounds. People cannot hear these high-pitched sounds. When the sounds hit an object, they bounce back to the bat's ears. The time the sounds take to get back to the bat's ears tells the bat how far away the object is. This is also how an echo works. It is how bats can find and catch flying insects in the dark.

The ability to use echoes to locate objects is called **echolocation**. All microbats can use echolocation. Only one species of megabat can use echolocation. It is the Rousettus fruit bat. Since most megabats cannot use echolocation, they find food using their excellent senses of smell and sight.

Bats **adapt** very well. Scientists think that the first bats ate insects during the day. They think some bats, however, changed and hunted at night because insect hunting was better then. Bats could avoid their enemies more easily if they slept during the day. Over time, all bats became nocturnal.

A scientist is measuring the size of these hibernating bats.

A bat's life cycle

Bats mate only once a year. Most bats give birth to one young per year, although some species have twins. Young bats are called **pups**.

Male and female bats mate in autumn, but their young are not born until spring. If bats live in cold areas, they **hibernate**. Hibernation is a deep sleep that lasts all winter. Young bats are usually born about two months after the mother comes out of hibernation. Some bats are born up to eight months after the mother's hibernation ends.

In many bat species, females go to a cave where other female bats have gathered before giving birth. Then they all have their young together. The male bats find homes somewhere else.

These pups are waiting for their mothers to return from hunting.

Young bats

Megabat pups are born with their eyes open wide. They are covered in fur. Most microbat pups are born with their eyes closed. They have pink skin and will not grow fur for at least a week.

Did you know that bats try to help other bats? When some mother bats find a young bat with no mother, they will take care of it. They have been known to give up their own food to share it with more hungry bats.

Fruit-eating mother bats carry their pups with them when they search for food. Mother bats that eat insects usually leave their young at home. When a mother bat returns from hunting, she must find her pup. She can recognize her pup by its chirping sounds and by its scent.

Bat pups drink milk from their mothers. Most microbats drink milk for one or two months. Large bats may drink milk for five months.

Most bats are almost fully grown after six weeks. That is when they learn how to fly. At first, they just flap their wings. Then they take short trips. As they get better, their trips get longer. By the end of summer, the young bats are expert flyers. It is time for them to go out at night and hunt for their own food.

Most bats live for about 15 years, but some live for more than 30 years. Most other small mammals, such as mice, live only a year or two.

These flying foxes are leaving their roost to look for food.

What is a bat's day like?

When the sun sets at night, bats wake up and leave their **roosts**. A roost is a place where a winged animal sleeps and rests. Bats leave their roosts to hunt for food.

Bats know their hunting areas well. They have a very good memory and good eyesight.

If they need to, they can fly without using their echolocation. It can be hard for a bat to echolocate if it has food in its mouth.

Some bats are good at flying through the forest. Other bats like to fly higher. The straw-coloured fruit bat flies as high as 2000 metres above the ground.

Some bats migrate. This means they travel great distances to find the best food and weather. Bats that migrate are often those that fly very high. The red bat migrates back and forth between Canada and Mexico.

Bats have to be careful because some animals in the rainforest are **predators**. Predators are animals that hunt other animals and eat them. The animals that predators hunt and eat are called **prey**. Owls can snatch bats out of the sky.

Before the sun rises, bats fly back to their roosts to sleep. If the bat has a pup, it will feed it before going to sleep. It is important for bats to be careful of predators, even when they are sleeping. Snakes can climb into trees or caves to catch bats. That is why bats choose roosts that hide them from other animals.

This bat is hunting for food at night.

Bats in the world today

Bats first appeared on Earth about 50 million years ago. Today they make up about 25 per cent of all mammal species. They have survived so long because they adapted well when their surroundings changed. They became able to hunt at night. They developed wings and became able to fly. They also developed echolocation.

Many people think bats are blind, but this is a myth. A myth is something that many people believe, even though it is not true. Bats actually see very well. Another myth about bats is that they get tangled in people's hair. This is not true either.

Scientists are studying the brains of bats. A bat's brain is quite like a human's brain. Scientists hope that understanding more about bat brains can help them understand more about humans.

25

Scientists teach other people about bats so that they do not fear these creatures.

Bats in danger

Even though there are billions of bats in the world, they are still in danger of dying out. People are cutting down trees in the rainforest to build roads and buildings. They are also selling the wood from the rainforest. Bats are losing their habitats. A habitat is a place where a plant or animal usually lives.

Many people kill bats because they have wrong ideas about them. They may poison or shoot bats. Sometimes they destroy bats' homes. These people think all bats carry diseases or are dangerous to people. The truth is that bats are very clean and rarely carry diseases. Bats actually try to avoid people.

Another reason bats are dying out is because they give birth to only one pup per year. Most pups die during their first year. They are either not strong enough to live, or they are killed by predators. Bats do not have enough young each year to replace the number of bats that die. Over time there will be fewer bats.

Some people are trying to save bats. They are trying to teach people not to believe myths and not to be afraid of bats. These people know that learning more about bats is one of the best ways to help save them. This will help keep bats alive in their rainforest homes for a very long time.

furry body
see pages 12, 13

sensitive ears
see page 17

eyes
see pages 9, 25

large wings
see page 13

Glossary

adapt when something changes to be a better fit in its environment

camouflage colours, shapes and patterns that help an animal blend in with its surroundings

echolocation (EK-oh-loh-KAY-shun) when a bat uses high-pitched sounds and echoes to find its way and hunt in the dark

hibernate to spend the winter in a deep sleep

mammal warm-blooded animal with fur and a backbone

membrane very thin layer of skin or tissue

nocturnal active at night

pollinator animal that spreads pollen so that new plants can grow

predator animal that hunts other animals and eats them

prey animal that predators hunt and eat

pup newborn or young bat

roost place where birds or bats sleep, rest or build their homes

Internet sites

Bat Conservation Trust
www.bats.org.uk

Eurobats
www.eurobats.org

Useful address

Bat Conservation Trust
15 Cloisters House
Battersea Park Road
LONDON   SW8 4BG

Books to read

Theodorou, Rod. *Animals in Danger: Grey Bat.*
Heinemann Library, Oxford, 2002.

Theodorou, R; Telford, C. *Amazing Journeys:
Up a Rainforest Tree.* Heinemann Library,
Oxford, 1998

Index